The Wonder Rocks

Written and Illustrated by Roger Blonder

The Wonder Rocks

Book design and art direction by Roger Blonder
Text set in Tobi Pro

ObservaStory™ Books
www.observastory.com

First Edition

ISBN 978-0-9776726-5-3

To Renée, Jaelyn and Noa,
I know it's not easy to see the world through my eyes.
Thank you for always trying.

I love you.

What brings you to the desert?
Are you here to camp and climb?
Or have you come to stargaze,
or to ponder life and time?

The desert is a playground
packed with more than fun and games.
Come **Wonderwalk** the **Land of Rocks**.
Hear their stories.
Learn their names.

Each one offers wisdom.
Each has a tale to tell.
Time to meet them.
Time to greet them.
Time to fall under their spell...

Rocky, **Squat** and **Bugeye**
are pals with **Bob** the **Shark**.
Protectors of the Desert.
Defenders of the Park.

They stand and keep a watchful eye
over sacred land and sky.
Go gently on the ground they guard:
Our monumental shared backyard.

Berty sits out in the field.
She's always being watched by **Tad**.
She sees and hears a lot of things
that make her kind of *sad*.

Like people dropping litter,
or lost inside their phones,
instead of trying to listen
to the ***Voices of the Stones***.

Is he scary?
Is she kind?
What's the story in your mind?

When you see those
BIG SHARP TEETH
Do you want to run away?

Or could you say with courage,
"Please don't eat me.
Wanna play?"

To wait in line is never fun.
Just try it in the desert sun
for one hundred million years
of *meta-phoric-morphic* tears.

To learn this kind of patience,
can* drive *you* crazy *mad.
But when you queue with **Neb** and **Shmoo**,
you'll find it's not so bad!

Hobart has a *humble heart.*
He's the sweetest hunk in town.
He's always here to listen
to your troubles when you're down.

So when you need a **boulder**
to rest your head and cry,
just come and spill your sorrow
into his *soulful eyes.*

He will *feel* you. He will *heal* you.
He will help to make you *whole.*
He will *hold* you and *console* you
and restore your broken soul.

When you're feeling **sad** and **grumpy**
and you want to **sit** and **pout**,
Just search within the shadows
for a friend to help you out.

Sometimes all it takes to make
new friends is just a smile.
Feeling shy? Why not try?
Might prove to be worthwhile!

Take a breath.
Rest your wings.
Spend some time alone.
Soon enough you'll need to fly.
For now,
be still
as stone.

A field of stone,
a perfect bed,
to rest a sweet and heavy head.

Red-tailed hawks and sunny days.

The neighbors gawk.
The lovers gaze.

A midday nap can help you find
some peace and solace in your mind.
What better place to seek repose
than on the bridge of **Berta's Nose?**

Absorbing waves of tranquil slumber ~~~
from sun-drenched hues of golden umber.

Sproffle, Wob and **Spiny**
are three playful, peppy jokers.
Just be careful not to get too close
to their pointy pokers.

Look.
Don't touch.
Or maybe try?
It might not hurt.
You might not cry.

Just can't help it.
Need to know...

"OUCH!"

Ha Ha!

I told you so!

Love is in the air today ~
All shapes and sizes on display.
How sweet it is when two souls find
their hearts are beating intertwined.

Maybe standing next to you
you'll find your perfect match.
Try to keep an open mind.
That **HUNK** is quite a catch!

In this rocky Hidden Valley,
if you're feeling lost and small,
heed this lesson from the **Courtly Cow**
who stands above it all:

Stumble through the rough terrain.
Scramble over boulders.
Clamber to the overlook
from my granite shoulders.

Expand your field of vision
past the distant mountain range.
Remember you are not alone
and the only truth is change.

Worry not, you'll find your way.
Tomorrow or some far off day.
Today, be still, enjoy the view...

Perspective...
Patience...
Deep Breath...
Moo.

Now the sun is setting in the west
and your journey's end is near.
The sands of time are calling.
Did you listen? Can you hear?

The whistling winds and chirping birds
bear otherworldly wisdom words
that filter through these rocks and stones
to settle in your hearts and bones.

It might seem *odd* to talk to rocks,
to give the land **a voice**.
If there's one thing to remember,
It's that you have a choice:

You can shiver, shake and tremble,
dread the dark and fear the thunder,
Or you can lighten up this heavy world
with joy and wit and wonder...

Time to sense a little deeper.
Never know just what you'll find,
When you **WonderWalk**
in the **Land of Rocks**
that tumble in your mind.

Made in United States
North Haven, CT
26 April 2023

35920275R00020